History's Mysteries

Debatable Deaths

Gary L. Blackwood
with Terry Miller Shannon

Marshall Cavendish
Benchmark
New York

Marshall Cavendish Benchmark
99 White Plains Road
Tarrytown, NY 10591
www.marshallcavendish.us

Library of Congress Cataloging-in-Publication Data

Blackwood, Gary L.
    Debatable deaths / by Gary L. Blackwood with Terry Miller Shannon.
      p. cm. — (Benchmark rockets—history's mysteries)
    Includes bibliographical references and index.
    Summary: "Discusses the mysteries surrounding history's debatable deaths"—Provided by publisher.
    ISBN 978-0-7614-4355-1
1. Celebrities—Biography—Juvenile literature. 2. Celebrities—Death—Juvenile literature. 3. Death—Juvenile literature. 4. Death—Causes—Juvenile literature. I. Shannon, Terry Miller, 1951- II. Title.

CT105.B583 2009
920.02—dc22
[B]
2008052757

Publisher: Michelle Bisson
Editorial Development and Book Design: Trillium Publishing, Inc.

Photo research by Trillium Publishing, Inc.

Cover photo: Photo provided courtesy of Purdue University, from Purdue University Libraries' The George Palmer Putnam Collections of Amelia Earhart Papers (Earhart); Jacques-Louis David, 1812 (Napoleon).

The photographs and illustrations in this book are used by permission and through the courtesy of: *iStockphoto.com*: Ken Pilon (rectangular frame), front cover, back cover, 1, 3, 9; Eliza Snow (oval frame), front cover, 1. *Purdue University*: Purdue University Libraries' The George Palmer Putnam Collections of Amelia Earhart Papers, 1 (Earhart), 22, 24. *Jacques-Louis David*: 1 (Napoleon), 18. *The Egypt Archive*: Jon Bodsworth, 5. *Corbis*: Hulton-Deutsch Collection, 6; The Art Archive, 10. *Siemens*: Press Picture, 8. *The Granger Collection, New York*: Rue des Archives, 12. *Independence National Historical Park*: 14. *Charles de Steuben*: 21. *Sunny Gagliano*: 27.

Printed in Malaysia
1 3 5 6 4 2

Contents

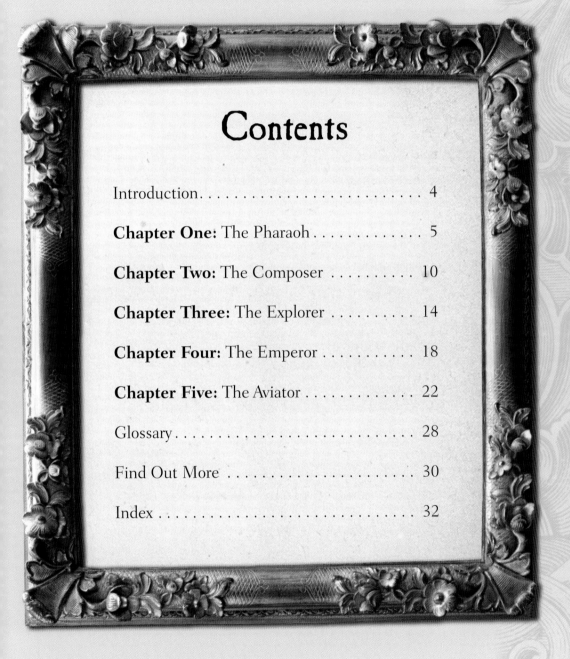

Introduction

Murder. The word is chilling. A death that could be a murder is mysterious and scary. No matter how long ago the death happened, we must uncover the truth. But can we?

A detective working on a fresh case can look at a body. Witnesses and suspects are there to tell what happened. These clues help solve the case.

Figuring out deaths that happened long ago is more difficult. We cannot ask dead suspects and witnesses questions. We rely on statements written back then. But these are not always complete. Sometime the statements don't agree with each other.

If we find the body, it may be too old to offer clues. Sometimes, though, we are lucky. We find clues that can be tested with modern tools.

The deaths in this book may not be murders. Many historians do not believe these deaths were the result of crimes. Should we just accept what everyone else thinks? History is filled with hidden murders. At one time, people often killed enemies. Murder can be hidden—for centuries.

We must dig into the past. We must question what people accept as true. When we question history, we can learn from it.

CHAPTER ONE

The Pharaoh

Egypt's rulers began building tombs underground around 1550 BC. The tombs were in an area now called the Valley of the Kings. The graves were kept secret to prevent them from being robbed.

Even though the tombs were secret, thieves found them. British **archaeologists** began digging there in the late 1800s. They found that people had already stolen from most of the graves.

In 1922, a man named Howard Carter dug in the area. He found what one expert calls "the richest discovery in the history of archaeology." It was a tomb that thieves had mostly left alone.

Very valuable art filled the tomb. Some of the pieces were made of solid gold. The grave also held a mummy. It was the preserved body of a young **pharaoh** named Tutankhamen. In the 1920s, no one knew anything about this young pharaoh.

Since then, scientists have found clues to Tutankhamen's life. They fit the clues together to form a rough picture of him. The experts think he was the son of Akhenaten and was originally called Tutankhaten.

Akhenaten is sometimes called "the **heretic** king." He rejected the Egyptians' common belief in many gods, and worshipped only the sun god Aten. He took the name Akhen<u>aten</u> to honor Aten. This name means "it is **beneficial** to Aten." He named his son Tutankh<u>aten</u>. Giving his son this name was another way Akhenaten honored the sun god.

Akhenaten's queen was Nefertiti. When Akhenaten died, Tutankhaten was four or five. A mysterious person named Smenkhare, who may have been Nefertiti, ruled the country for the next two years. Then Tutankhaten became pharaoh.

By the time Howard Carter began digging in the Valley of the Kings, most of the tombs had been cleaned out by thieves or archaeologists.

Tutankhaten's main adviser was Lord Ay, Akhenaten's uncle. Ay suggested that Tutankhaten bring back the old religion of believing in many gods. The young pharaoh restored the old religion and changed his name to Tutankhamen. This name honors Amen, one of the old gods.

Tutankhamen married his half sister, Ankhesenamen. In 1323 BC, Tutankhamen died suddenly. He was just 17 years old. His tomb was not finished, so he was buried in a smaller, plainer tomb.

Tutankhamen had no children to take over his rule, so Ay took the throne. Ay probably tried to marry Ankhesenamen. His right to rule would be stronger if he were married to Tutankhamen's widow.

It seems Ankhesenamen did not want to marry Ay. She sent a message to the king of the **Hittites**, Egypt's enemy. She said she would not marry a **commoner**. (Ay was not of royal blood.) She asked if she could marry one of the Hittite king's sons. One son wanted to marry Ankhesenamen and become a pharaoh. On the way to Egypt, however, he was attacked and killed.

In 1931, a ring was found. The names of Ay and Ankhesenamen are engraved on it. The names are linked together. Some experts think Ay married Ankhesenamen to make his claim to the throne stronger. Then he killed her. If Ay was that cruel, he may also have killed Tutankhamen to become pharaoh.

Tutankhamen's skull was X-rayed in 1969. The X rays showed a thinned bone behind the left ear. This could have been caused by a blow to the head. Ay is one suspect, but there are others. A general named Horemheb took the throne after Ay died. Horemheb hated Tutankhamen and his father. Some of his people thought he had murdered Tutankhamen.

Some experts do not believe Tutankhamen was murdered. A **CT scan** of the mummy in 2005 convinced many experts that Tutankhamen did not die from a blow to his head. Some day we may know more. Until then, Tutankhamen's death remains a mystery. ✖

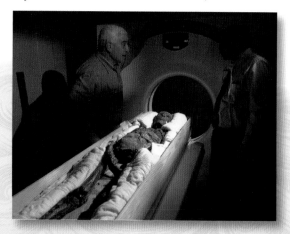

This CT scan of Tutankhamen's mummy provided more clues to the cause of his death.

The Pharaoh's Curse

The discovery of Tutankhamen's tomb caused excitement—and panic. Stories spread of a pharaoh's curse. They began when Howard Carter was digging up the tomb. A cobra ate his pet canary. The snake was a symbol of the pharaohs.

Later, a newspaper printed a letter that predicted doom for Carter's group. The letter included a warning that was supposed to be from an old Egyptian book: "Death comes on wings to him who enters the tomb of a Pharaoh."

Then, the man who paid Carter to dig died in Cairo. Doctors said he died from an infected mosquito bite. But two strange things happened. The lights in Cairo went out the moment he died. At the same time, his dog howled and dropped dead in England.

Over the next several years, more than 20 people who visited the tomb died, including two of Carter's helpers. Scientists said the deaths could have had many causes. The tomb may have held germs or poison.

In 1980, the last living member of Carter's team shared a secret. Carter started the curse story himself. He wanted to keep visitors and robbers away from the tomb.

CHAPTER TWO

The Composer

It is not so hard to imagine a king being killed. Politicians and royal families have always had enemies and rivals. It is harder, however, to imagine why anyone would want to kill a man who gave the world some of its most delightful music.

Wolfgang Amadeus Mozart was born in Austria in 1756 and became a child musical star. He started playing the harpsichord when he was four years old. When he was only five, he wrote two **minuets**. At age six, he played for the Austrian emperor. Mozart wrote his first **sonata** at age seven, followed by his first **symphony** when he was eight. He wrote his first **opera** at age 12. Mozart was only 35 years old when he died. It is lucky that he got such an early start on his musical career.

Unlike many child stars, Mozart more than lived up to his promise. His music was very popular. He composed many pieces of music. In 1787 the emperor hired him as the court composer. But his pay was so low that he was very poor. He often had to beg his friends to lend him money.

No one envied Mozart for his money. But many envied his talent. A composer named Antonio Salieri was very jealous of Mozart. Salieri was also popular. He taught many musicians who became famous, such as Beethoven. Salieri had a huge **ego**. One writer wrote that Salieri wanted to be the only successful composer of his time.

Salieri tried to stop the production of one of Mozart's operas in 1782. The emperor made sure the opera was performed. It was a big success. That success made Salieri even more bitter.

Three years later, Salieri tried to stop another Mozart opera. He told the performers that the music was impossible to sing. The performers, however, loved Mozart's music. Salieri failed again.

Mozart's opera *The Magic Flute* had its first performance in 1791. By then, Salieri was over his envy, or at least he hid it well. He went to the opera with Mozart. Afterward, Mozart said "Salieri listened and watched most attentively. . . ."

That November, Mozart suddenly fell ill. One writer said it began when his hands and feet swelled up. He could not move and began to vomit. The great composer died on December 5, 1791.

At the time, officials said Mozart died of a fever. Today, many experts think he died of **kidney** disease. Others believe he died of **rheumatic fever** or an infection. At least one expert thinks undercooked pork made him sick.

Mozart believed something else made him sick. Before he died he told his wife someone had poisoned him with **arsenic**. Others believed the same thing. A newspaper reported that some people thought he'd been poisoned because of the way his body swelled up after he died.

In the last months of his life, Mozart began writing a requiem, or mass for the dead. He continued working on the piece as he lay dying.

Mozart's son said his father's body was too bloated for an **autopsy**. The body was soft and flexible, which are signs of poisoning.

If Mozart was poisoned, Salieri would be a suspect. He even said Mozart's death was a blessing for other composers. By 1824 so many people believed he killed Mozart that a concert program showed him standing by Mozart's bed with a cup of poison. Stories spread that Salieri confessed to the murder and then tried to kill himself. Salieri denied these stories.

Someone else may have poisoned Mozart. Some experts think he was killed by a group he belonged to, called the **Freemasons**. They say members of the group killed him because he showed their secret **rituals** in *The Magic Flute*. This seems unlikely, though. Mozart wrote his opera to defend the Freemasons.

Other experts think a Freemason named Franz Hofdemel killed Mozart. Hofdemel's wife was a student of Mozart's. Hofdemel argued with his wife the day after Mozart died. He cut his wife's face and body. Then he killed himself. His wife never said why they argued. Some people suggest she had a romance with Mozart, and her husband found out.

In 1983, a mock trial was held to look at the possible reasons Mozart died. The audience decided he had been killed. They believed Franz Hofdemel was his murderer.

CHAPTER THREE

The Explorer

Modern tests can help decide the cause of a death decades or even centuries later. To conduct these tests, however, scientists need something to work with. We know where Meriwether Lewis lies. Testing his body might clear up the mystery of his death. The tests might show if he killed himself or was murdered.

Meriwether Lewis is famous for exploring the Louisiana Purchase. The United States bought the territory of Louisiana from France in 1803. Back then, Louisiana covered 828,000 square miles. It stretched from New Orleans along the Mississippi River to what is now Montana. Buying it doubled the country's size.

President Thomas Jefferson picked Lewis to lead the Corps of Discovery. This group explored the Louisiana Purchase from 1804–1806. By 1808, Lewis was the governor of the Upper Louisiana Territory.

Lewis was a good governor by most accounts, but he ran into money problems. Lewis needed money to prepare a team to return a Mandan Indian chief to his home. He asked for money from the War Department in Washington, D.C. He was refused.

Lewis was already around four thousand dollars in debt. The people he owed money to wanted it back. Lewis faced going broke.

He decided to go to Washington, D.C., to work out his problems with the War Department. He may have had other plans as well, such as stressing his loyalty to the country. Some people said that Lewis planned to make land west of the Mississippi River into a new nation. They claimed that when he returned the Mandan chief to his home, his real goal was to explore more land.

Some historians think Lewis had yet another reason to go to Washington. They think he wanted to speak against General James Wilkinson. Wilkinson was also accused of planning to make the land west of the Mississippi River into a separate nation. In addition, he sold government secrets to Spain.

On September 4, 1809, Lewis began his journey to Washington, leaving St. Louis by boat. He fell ill. Crew members said he tried to kill himself. They carried him ashore at Fort Pickering, near what is now Memphis, Tennessee.

Fort commander Captain Gilbert Russell was alarmed at how ill Lewis was. He said Lewis acted crazy. Russell refused to let Lewis leave until he was well. Lewis took some medicine and was much better in a week or so.

Lewis changed his travel plans while at Fort Pickering. Fearing his ship might be attacked by the British, he decided to ride horses along a trail called the **Natchez Trace**. The trail could be dangerous, but his servant, Pernia, went with him. So did a Chickasaw Indian agent named Major James Neelly, who also brought his slave and several Chickasaws.

They traveled for over a week. On October 10, 1809, two of the horses ran off. Neelly stayed to find them, planning to meet Lewis later.

Lewis rode on to Grinder's Stand, a tiny settlement. Robert Grinder was away. Priscilla Grinder rented a cabin to Lewis and cooked for him. Lewis paced, talked to himself, and did not eat.

Our only information about what happened next comes from Priscilla Grinder. Her stories were not written down, and they changed over time. When Neelly arrived, Lewis was dead. Mrs. Grinder told Neelly that she heard two pistols fire. Lewis lived long enough to say, "I have done the business. . . ."

Priscilla Grinder told another story to a scientist named Alexander Wilson in 1811. She said she heard a shot and then something heavy fell. Then she heard another shot. Lewis asked for help before he died.

Thirty years later, Mrs. Grinder told a traveling teacher yet another story. In this tale, two or three men arrived after dark. Lewis challenged them to a duel. The men left. The rest of the story is much the same as the story Wilson heard. In this one, though, Pernia appeared wearing Lewis's clothes. This suggests that Pernia stole from Lewis after he died.

Experts draw different conclusions from these stories. Some think the strangers were outlaws who came back to rob and kill Lewis. Others think Pernia or Neelly stole from Lewis. Both said he owed them money, and Neelly kept Lewis's guns and horse after his death.

Some people think Mrs. Grinder's husband killed Lewis. Robert Grinder was known for his violent acts. Others think General Wilkinson had Lewis killed. Some say he was robbed because he carried a map to a gold mine. Many believe Lewis killed himself. However, people wonder why a gun expert such as Lewis would not be able to kill himself instantly.

A **forensic** science professor wants to dig up the grave at Grinder's Stand to examine Lewis's body. Many of Lewis's **descendants** support him. The professor began asking the National Park Service for permission in 1996. So far, the Park Service has refused.

CHAPTER FOUR

The Emperor

People may suspect murder even after a doctor studies a body and says the person died of natural causes. One of these cases is that of Napoleon Bonaparte. The **exiled** French emperor died May 5, 1821, at age 51. Seven doctors examined his body. Their report said he died of stomach cancer.

Now some experts think the doctors made a mistake. Or, since he died in British territory, they just told British authorities what they wanted to hear.

Napoleon came to power during the **French Revolution**. He declared himself Emperor of the French in 1804. He was not happy to just rule France. He began invading his neighbor countries. Some of the countries, including Britain, joined together to become **allies** and fight against him.

In 1814 the allies defeated Napoleon. The victors forced him to give up his crown. They sent him away to the island of Elba. A year later, he returned to France. The allies defeated Napoleon again. This time, the allies sent him away to Saint Helena.

Saint Helena, a small island off Africa, was controlled by Britain. It was damp and ugly. In spite of the mold growing on the walls of his house and the rats under the table where he ate, Napoleon had a good life. He had servants. He enjoyed good health. Friends came to visit.

Then Saint Helena got a new governor in April 1816. The governor's name was Sir Hudson Lowe. Lowe treated Napoleon like a prisoner. Napoleon said Lowe had come to kill him.

There may have been some truth in his belief. According to one historian, the British government had paid a secret group whose purpose was to kill Napoleon. The leader, the comte d'Artois, would later become France's King Charles X.

There's no proof, however, that Lowe was part of a plot to kill Napoleon. Soon after Lowe arrived, though, Napoleon began to get sick. He became weak. His head hurt. He had chills and pain. His speech slurred. He acted like he had been drugged.

Lowe did not believe that Napoleon was sick. He thought Napoleon was faking illness in the hope that he would be moved to a nicer place. A doctor said he had a liver disease. Lowe refused to believe the doctor. He hired another doctor, who said Napoleon was in no danger.

Napoleon remained ill. He had fevers and was sick to his stomach. He said he was being poisoned. Later, he decided he was dying from stomach cancer.

The doctors' autopsy report supported Napoleon's opinion, but it left out some important information. The doctors present when Napoleon's body was examined did not all agree with each other. The report did not mention that one doctor said Napoleon's liver was too big. A large liver could mean he had a liver disease—or that he had been poisoned. It is possible that Governor Lowe did not want the large liver mentioned in the report.

Napoleon was buried on Saint Helena. Nineteen years later, his body was moved to France. It was perfectly preserved. High levels of arsenic could preserve the body. Some saw this as proof that he had been poisoned.

In 1960, a Swedish scientist tested Napoleon's hair. He found large amounts of arsenic. He believed someone close to Napoleon had poisoned him at the request of the comte d'Artois.

In 1980, a British chemist had a new idea. He tested a scrap of wallpaper from the room in which Napoleon died. He found that the color in the paper contained arsenic. When the paper grew damp and moldy, it would have given off a poisonous gas. The gas would have been **toxic** enough to make Napoleon sick.

More recently, a lab tested a piece of Napoleon's hair from before he went to Saint Helena. That hair had high levels of arsenic, too. Some think he may have poisoned himself with a hair **tonic**. Back then, people used arsenic in different medicines and tonics. Napoleon could have poisoned himself without knowing it.

Napoleon died in this room. The wallpaper in the picture matches the wallpaper that the chemist tested.

CHAPTER FIVE

The Aviator

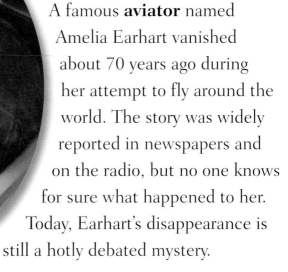

A famous **aviator** named Amelia Earhart vanished about 70 years ago during her attempt to fly around the world. The story was widely reported in newspapers and on the radio, but no one knows for sure what happened to her. Today, Earhart's disappearance is still a hotly debated mystery.

No one thinks twice about flying now. When Earhart began flying in the 1920s, however, flying was a new and amazing way to travel. People thought pilots were daring pioneers. Charles Lindbergh finished the first solo nonstop flight across the Atlantic in 1927. This flight made him an instant hero.

In 1928, Earhart was the first woman to cross the Atlantic by air. She was just a passenger, but the trip still made her famous. She would become more famous in future years.

Earhart set a world speed record for women pilots. She was the first woman to fly solo across the Atlantic and the first woman to fly nonstop across North America. Earhart was the first pilot—male or female—to fly alone from Hawaii to the mainland of the United States and from Mexico City to New York.

Earhart also spoke out for women's rights. She hoped for a time "when women will know no restrictions because of sex but will be individuals free to live their lives as men are free."

By the time she was 40 years old, Earhart was one of the world's most admired women. But she wanted to make one last grand trip. She wanted to be sure of a place in flying history. She decided she would be the first woman pilot to make the 25,000-mile trip around the world. She told a reporter that she believed she had one more good flight left. When it was done, she would quit long-distance flying.

At first, she planned to make the trip alone. But she realized her **navigating** skills were not strong enough for the journey. She took an experienced navigator named Harry Manning.

Earhart's plane was a twin-engine Lockheed Electra. It was fitted with extra fuel tanks. She could fly a distance of around 2,500 to 3,000 miles before needing to refuel. She planned to fly west from California. But it is 7,000 miles across the Pacific Ocean from North America to **New Guinea**. She would need to stop for more fuel during that part of the trip. Luckily, Earhart could use the airstrip on Howland Island. Howland was about halfway across the ocean.

After taking off from California, Earhart shortened the distance between fuel stops even more by landing in Hawaii. But when she took off again, her plane swung sideways. Earhart turned too quickly the other way. Her landing gear broke. She blamed the problem on bad equipment. She continued to believe in her own skills.

Her second try at her big flight around the world started on May 20, 1937. She flew east this time from Oakland, California. Manning refused to travel with her. He complained that she was bossy. Fred Noonan went instead. Noonan was an experienced navigator, but he had a problem with alcohol.

From left: Amelia Earhart, Harry Manning, and Fred Noonan

Earhart and Noonan made a series of short flights. It took them more than a month to reach New Guinea. Earhart was very tired. Noonan was drinking too much. They rested for two days. Then, on July 2, they took off for Howland Island.

A strong headwind caused them to use fuel much faster than they had planned. Their tanks would be nearly empty when they landed on Howland. If they missed the island, they knew they would be in trouble.

They had a two-way radio and a **direction finder**. But neither one knew how to use this equipment. The Coast Guard ship *Itasca* waited near Howland Island to help guide them. Earhart sent messages to the ship, but she used the wrong frequency on the radio. The Coast Guard could barely hear her. Earhart didn't receive most of the Coast Guard's messages.

The plane never reached Howland. Noonan might have been feeling ill from drinking. He may have calculated wrong. If he gave Earhart the right directions, she might have ignored him. She had ignored him before while flying over the Atlantic.

Nineteen hours after Earhart left New Guinea, the Coast Guard got a clear message from her. Earhart said, "We must be on you but cannot see you but gas is running low." An hour later, she radioed their position: "We are on the line of position one five seven dash three three seven. . . . We are running north and south."

That was the last anyone ever heard from Earhart and Noonan—at least officially.

The Coast Guard and the Navy searched 250,000 square miles of ocean. They searched the Gilbert Islands, in case Earhart landed north. The search found no sign of the plane or its crew.

The Coast Guard did not search the **Marshall Islands**, which are north of the Gilbert Islands, because they were controlled by Japan. When the United States went to war with Japan four years later, a story spread that President Roosevelt had asked Earhart to spy on the Japanese during her flight. Some people believed this story because Earhart was flying so close to Japanese territory. The government denied it.

In 1960, a woman named Josephine Blanco Akiyama told a startling story. Akiyama grew up on the island of **Saipan**, which was controlled by Japan. She saw a twin-engine plane land in the harbor in the summer of 1937. She said that Japanese soldiers brought in a tall man and a short-haired American woman dressed like a man. They took them into the woods. Shots rang out. The soldiers returned alone.

In 1944–1945, Americans controlled Saipan. One soldier saw a plane like Earhart's. He asked the guard if it was hers. The guard said yes. Later, a woman showed him the grave of two white people who had "come from the sky" and been killed by the Japanese.

A former Japanese **medic** also said he saw a plane that seemed to be Earhart's. It was on a Japanese ship headed to Saipan. He had gone on board the ship to care for two injured English-speaking prisoners. The crew called the woman prisoner "Meel-ya."

Many people believe Earhart went down in the Marshall Islands. Others don't agree. In 1970, a writer claimed a New Jersey woman was Earhart. The woman denied it.

A group that saves old planes thinks Earhart crash-landed on or near Gardner Island. They have searched the island several times but have found no proof.

In 2002, the team that found the *Titanic* looked for Earhart's plane on the ocean floor near

The map shows Lae, New Guinea, where Earhart started her flight; Howland Island, where the plane was to refuel; and Saipan, where some people reported seeing a captured woman pilot.

Howland Island. They could not find it. Amelia Earhart's disappearance continues to be a mystery. ✻

Glossary

allies: Countries that join together for a common purpose.

archaeologists: Scientists who study past human life and culture.

arsenic: A poisonous element that was used to treat infections, harden metals, and kill insects.

autopsy: An exam done on a dead person to find the cause of death.

aviator: A person who flies an airplane.

beneficial: Helps or provides advantages.

commoner: A person who is not of noble rank.

CT scan: An image of a body part made by a computer using X-ray images.

descendants: A person's children, grandchildren, great-grandchildren, and so on.

direction finder: Equipment that helps pilots find their location by using radio signals sent from the ground.

ego: Sense of self-worth. A person with a huge ego has too much pride in himself or herself.

exiled: Sent away from his or her country, and ordered not to return.

forensic: Using science to help solve crimes.

Freemasons: A group that promotes peace and service to others.

French Revolution: A violent uprising in France from 1789–1799.

heretic: Someone whose views are different from a certain religion or not acceptable to authorities.

Hittites: An ancient group of people who destroyed the city of Babylon around 1600 BC. They then set up a powerful empire that included most of what is now Turkey and Syria. Their empire was destroyed by invaders around 1200 BC.

kidney: One of the pair of organs that remove waste from blood, turning it into urine.

medic: Someone trained to give medical help.

minuets: Ballroom dances common in the eighteenth century.

Marshall Islands: A group of 34 islands located 2,200 miles southwest of Hawaii. The Marshall Islands were Japanese territory from 1914 until 1944, when they were captured by the United States.

Natchez Trace: A road that crossed 500 miles of wilderness between Natchez, Mississippi, and Nashville, Tennessee.

navigating: Planning and controlling the course of an airplane.

New Guinea: The world's second largest island, located just north of Australia.

opera: A play in which all or most of the words are sung.

pharaoh: A king of ancient Egypt.

rheumatic fever: A serious disease that causes fever and joint pain and can damage the heart.

rituals: Acts or practices that take place in ceremonies.

Saipan: The second largest of the Mariana Islands.

sonata: A piece of music for one or two instruments that has three or four main parts.

symphony: A long piece of music for an orchestra.

tonic: A medicine that increases strength.

toxic: Poisonous, deadly.

Find Out More

Books

Blackwood, Gary L. *Debatable Deaths*. New York: Marshall Cavendish, 2006.

For readers who would like to know more about mysterious deaths, this book goes into more detail.

Greenblatt, Miriam. *Napoleon Bonaparte and Imperial France*. New York: Marshall Cavendish, 2006.

This book describes the life of Napoleon Bonaparte and the culture in which he lived.

Hawass, Zahi. *Tutankhamun: The Mystery of the Boy King*. New York: National Geographic Children's Books, 2005.

The author of this book is the Director of Excavations at the Giza Pyramids and the Valley of the Golden Mummies.

McDonough, Yona Zeldis. *Who Was Wolfgang Amadeus Mozart?* New York: Grosset & Dunlap, 2003.

This account of Mozart's life and amazing musical career also discusses the history of opera, how musical instruments have changed over time, and life in eighteenth century Europe.

Stone, Tanya. *Amelia Earhart*. New York: DK Publishing, 2007.

This book tells the story of Amelia Earhart from her childhood to the mystery of her disappearance. The book includes many photographs and a timeline.

Websites

http://www.ameliaearhartmuseum.org

This is the website of the Amelia Earhart Birthplace Museum in Atchison, Kansas.

http://www.pbs.org/empires/napoleon/n_myth/youth/page_1.html

This site provides a biography of Napoleon Bonaparte.

http://www.pbs.org/wnet/pharaohs/digging.html

Explore King Tutankhamen's tomb, view a timeline of the pharaohs, see maps of Egypt, and more in "Secrets of the Pharaohs."

Index

Page numbers for photographs and illustrations are in **boldface**.